WITHDRAWN

WHAT ARE B VITAMINS?

The term "vitamin B" actually refers to "vitamin B-complex", a group of eight closely related but chemically distinct vitamins that frequently work together to maintain health. Some B vitamins are referred to by their "B name", while others are better known by their chemical name. The B-complex vitamins are vitamin B1(thiamin), vitamin B2 (riboflavin), vitamin B3 (niacin), vitamin B5 (pantothenic acid), vitamin B6 (pyridoxine), vitamin B7 (biotin), vitamin B9 (folic acid or folate), and vitamin B12 (cobalamin). The B vitamins act as co-factors in protein, fatty acid, and carbohydrate metabolism, and maintain a range of body functions. They are therefore essential components of the diet and help to maintain good health. Deficiency can result in a range of conditions affecting skin, blood, and the nervous system.

The B-complex vitamins share other characteristics. All are water-soluble, meaning that instead of storing unused amounts of these vitamins, the body excretes whatever it doesn't use. Absorption of B vitamins can be reduced when gut inflammation exists. This problem is particularly common in older people, so as people get older there is a greater need to ensure that intake is adequate. Other groups that are particularly susceptible to deficiency are pregnant and lactating women as they have increased needs, vegetarians, as one of the vitamins, B12, is only found in animal foods, and alcoholics, who may have a poor diet. The B-complex vitamins are found in a range of foods, including brewer's yeast, cereals – particularly whole grains, offal, dairy produce, nuts, and leafy green vegetables.

· VITAMIN B SUPPLEMENTS ·

For individuals who need help in getting enough vitamin B-complex, supplements are important. But to take eight pills at one time can be daunting. A better option is a vitamin B-complex supplement that contains all eight vitamins. Look for a product that contains at least the minimum RDA (recommended daily allowances) for each separate nutrient.

HOW MUCH DO I TAKE?

How many times have you stood in front of the vitamin shelves in your local health food store or pharmacy and compared labels? And how many times have you wondered why one brand offers 60mg of vitamin C when another boasts 750mg? Or why another product has 180mcg of folate when a competing brand features 400mcg of the same nutrient? And perhaps more importantly, which one is better? When it comes to dosages, there is no magic number. Requirements for nutrients are set by The Department of Health. These recommended amounts are known as Dietary Reference Values (DRVs) and act as a guide to the amounts needed to avoid nutritional deficiency diseases such as beriberi, rickets, or scurvy. However, many researchers, medical experts, and health authorities believe that the body needs much higher levels of vitamins for optimum health. And in the presence of illness, pollution, prescription medication, or stress, the body may need still higher levels. For this reason, throughout this book, we suggest a range of vitamin dosages. To determine the best level for you, consult your doctor first.

VITAMIN B1(THIAMIN)

Up until the 1930s thousands of people in south-east Asia died each year of a central nervous system disease called beriberi. The disease damaged nerves, leaving victims mentally impaired, crippled, paralyzed, or dead. In 1936 scientists discovered a substance in food that prevented the disease. The substance was named thiamin, also known as vitamin B1, and soon commercially milled flours were enriched with the vitamin.

Vitamin B1 plays an essential role in carbohydrate metabolism, so recommended intakes are based on energy or calorie intakes. However, recommended amounts can be based on average calorie intakes (see page 7). The vitamin also interacts in various other metabolic pathways, resulting in B1 having an effect on a number of different organs and tissues in the body. In particular it is vital to the normal functioning of the nervous system, brain, heart, and lungs.

Grains such as these are now often enriched with vitamin B1 when they are ground into flour.

· DOSAGES ·

RECOMMENDED DOSAGE Men, 0.9mg/day; women, 0.8 mg/day;
pregnant women, 0.9mg/day (last trimester only).
No known toxicity of B1 or thiamin is known when taken orally.

DEFICIENCY SYMPTOMS Appetite loss, fatigue, gastrointestinal
disturbances, irregular heartbeat, irritability, muscle atrophy, nervousness,
numbness in hands and feet, poor coordination, weakness, and weight
loss. Acute vitamin B1 deficiency is known as beriberi and occurs in
malnourished individuals in many parts of Asia where refined rice is
the staple diet.

FOOD SOURCES Brewer's yeast, brown rice, egg yolks, fish, legumes,
peanuts, peas, pork, wheat germ, and whole grains. Vitamin B1 is
removed from cereals by refining. Much of the dietary source of the
vitamin in western diets is from fortified cereals.

SPECIAL NEEDS Vitamin B1 deficiency occurs because of inadequate
intake, poor absorption, or increased needs; people with chronic disease,
who may have a poor appetite or anorexia, alcoholics, or people with
gut problems or malabsorption have increased needs.

VITAMIN B2 (RIBOFLAVIN)

Although it is rare today, at one time the disease ariboflavinosis was often found among individuals with limited diets. Characterized by inflammation of the mouth and tongue, mouth sores, skin lesions, sore throat, and weakness, the disease was discovered to be caused by a deficiency of riboflavin, hence the disease's name.

Like other members of the B-vitamin family, riboflavin helps the body metabolize carbohydrates, fats, and proteins. Also known as vitamin B2, the nutrient is fundamental in red blood cell formation, and cell respiration. It facilitates the utilization of oxygen by the tissues of the skin, mucous membranes (including the mucous membranes of the digestive tract), nails, and hair. The vitamin interacts with other B vitamins, for instance, in the metabolism of niacin *(see page 10)*, also involving pyridoxine *(see page 14)*, resulting in a lack of specific symptoms for B2 or riboflavin deficiency. Poor appetite and malabsorption can precipitate deficiency.

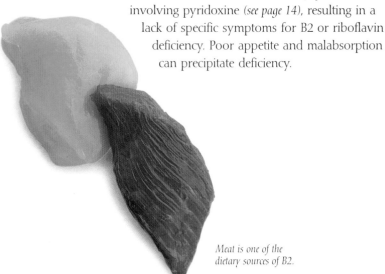

Meat is one of the dietary sources of B2.

· DOSAGES ·

RECOMMENDED DOSAGE Men, 1.7mg; women, 1.1mg; pregnant women, 1.4mg; lactating women, 1.6mg.
There is no evidence of riboflavin toxicity or therapeutic benefit at doses greater than those recommended.

DEFICIENCY SYMPTOMS Cracks at the corners of the mouth, dermatitis, itchy or burning eyes, light sensitivity, mouth sores, inflammation of the tongue, and rashes.

FOOD SOURCES Most plant and animal foods contain some vitamin B2. The principal sources are dairy products, including milk, cheese, and eggs. Other sources are poultry, meat, fish, asparagus, broccoli, and spinach. Unless fortified, cereals are a poor source of riboflavin.

SPECIAL NEEDS Chronic alcoholics and people with malabsorption or gut problems are at greater risk of deficiency. People with diabetes may also have increased needs because of high urinary excretion of the vitamin. The requirement for the vitamin may increase with physical activity. Higher intakes are recommended during pregnancy and while lactating.

VITAMIN B3 (NIACIN)

Pellagra was once a relatively common disease in the United States and Europe. Characterized by anxiety, chronic diarrhoea, dermatitis, progressive dementia, weakness, and weight loss, pellagra was most often observed among poor individuals who existed on a corn-based diet.

Although cereals such as oatmeal, rice, or wheat contain some niacin, with lesser amounts in corn, the availability of niacin from cereal varies. In addition, some traditional cooking methods can increase the availability. Niacin can be metabolized from tryptophan, an amino acid found in animal proteins. Good sources of tryptophan include meat and diary products. So a diet that is made up of a reasonable amount of animal protein can help to replace a deficiency of niacin or vitamin B3.

Niacin functions as a factor in numerous reactions involved in carbohydrate and fatty acid metabolism, tissue respiration and detoxification. It is used in large doses to treat people who have high levels of blood fats such as cholesterol and triglyceride. However, side effects such as flushing and an increased risk of peptic ulceration can reduce its application in high doses.

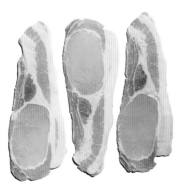

Bacon is a good source of niacin.

· DOSAGES ·

RECOMMENDED DOSAGE Men, 17mg; women, 13mg; pregnant women, 13mg; lactating women, 15mg. There is increased conversion of tryptophan to niacin during pregnancy.

DEFICIENCY SYMPTOMS Depression, fatigue, headaches, insomnia, limb pains, loss of appetite, low blood sugar, mouth sores, muscular weakness, and skin eruptions.

FOOD SOURCES Brewer's yeast, dairy products, meat, including pork, fortified cereals.

SPECIAL NEEDS Individuals who drink alcohol daily have increased needs for vitamin B3. Because they do not metabolize the vitamin efficiently, elderly people and individuals with hyperthyroidism also need higher levels of vitamin B3.

CAUTIONS Niacin deficiency occurs in Hartnup's disease, where absorption of several amino acids including tryptophan is impaired.

VITAMIN B5 (PANTOTHENIC ACID)

Vitamin B5 is also known as pantothenic acid. Like the other B-group vitamins, it is essential in reactions involved in the metabolism of carbohydrate, protein, and fat, including fatty acid synthesis and degradation, and steroid hormone synthesis. Human deficiency is rare but severely deficient diets result in dermatitis and "burning feet syndrome". It is required by all cells in the body and is involved in more than 100 different metabolic functions, including energy metabolism of carbohydrates, proteins, and lipids, the synthesis of lipids, neurotransmitters, steroid hormones, porphyrins, and haemoglobin. The vitamin helps build red blood cells, assists in making bile, and is necessary for the normal functioning of the gastrointestinal tract. It is also a stamina enhancer and has been found to be helpful in treating depression.

Broccoli

Asparagus

· DOSAGES ·

RECOMMENDED DOSAGE There is no recommended allowance for pantothenic acid but intakes of between 3 and 7mg/day appear to be safe for adults.

There are no specific therapeutic uses for pantothenic acid or reports of serious toxicity with excessive intakes of up to 10mg/day.

DEFICIENCY SYMPTOMS Vitamin B5 deficiency is extremely rare and is likely only to occur with starvation.

FOOD SOURCES Pantothenic acid is widely distributed in nature, especially in animal products, whole grains, and legumes. Natural sources include Brewer's yeast, meat, offal, brown rice, and pulses such as lentils and soya beans.

SPECIAL NEEDS None.

VITAMIN B6 (PYRIDOXINE)

Vitamin B6 occurs naturally in various forms and, like the other B-group vitamins, has a role in the metabolism of carbohydrate, protein, and fat. It acts as a co-factor in numerous reactions related to protein metabolism and requirements are therefore related to the amount of protein in the diet. The vitamin has a number of specific functions including the synthesis of niacin from tryptophan *(see page 10)*. It is also involved in the synthesis of red blood cells and plays a role in supporting the normal functioning of the nervous system. Several drugs produce pyridoxine deficiency by binding to one of its active forms and making it unavailable. Chronic alcoholism is one cause of pyridoxine deficiency and is due to a number of reasons, including poor diet and decreased release of the vitamin from food as well as increased excretion of the vitamin.

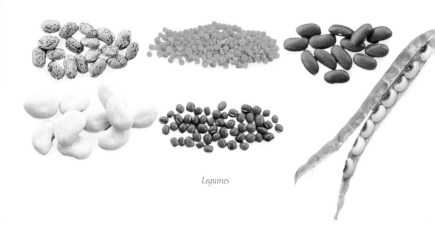

Legumes

· DOSAGES ·

RECOMMENDED DOSAGE Men, 1.4mg/day; women, 1.2mg/day;
pregnant women, 1.2mg/day. Pyridoxine should only be taken in cases
of deficiency in doses of 2-10mg/day. Severe toxicity has resulted from
taking large doses of pyridoxine; a severe sensory neuropathy of hands
and feet may develop with continued doses of 100-200mg/day.

DEFICIENCY SYMPTOMS Pyridoxine deficiency is rare. Symptoms
include inflammation of the tongue, lesions of the lips and corners of
the mouth and peripheral neuropathy.

FOOD SOURCES Poultry, port, fish, offal, eggs, soya beans, oats, peanuts,
walnuts, and unpolished rice are all good sources. The availability of
pyridoxine from different foods varies. Freezing and thawing may cause
significant loss of the vitamin.

SPECIAL NEEDS Pyridoxine deficiency may occur in people taking
certain drugs including levodopa and penicillame. Pyridoxine deficiency
has also been reported in some people undergoing dialysis for chronic
renal failure and in alcoholics. Individuals taking the oral contraceptive
pill may have increased needs.

VITAMIN B7 (BIOTIN)

Best known by many people as a moisturizing agent in shampoos, conditioners, and skin creams, biotin is essential to numerous body processes. As with other B vitamins, biotin allows the body to metabolize carbohydrates, fats, and proteins. Biotin is also a co-factor in fatty acid synthesis and metabolism.

Squid

Scallops

Fish

· DOSAGES ·

RECOMMENDED DOSAGE Although there are no recommended allowances, 10–20mcg/day are considered safe intakes for adults. There are no reports of toxicity of biotin in amounts up to 10mg/day.

DEFICIENCY SYMPTOMS Though biotin deficiency is rare, it can lead to fatigue, loss of appetite, depression, hair loss, lethargy, muscle pain, nausea, and skin rashes.

FOOD SOURCES Liver, egg yolk, soya flour, cereals, and yeast are rich sources. Fruit and meat are poor sources. The availability of biotin depends on binding agents in food. For instance, wheat contains biotin in an unavailable bound form. Although biotin is tightly bound to avidin in raw egg white, it is made available by cooking.

SPECIAL NEEDS People on total parenteral nutrition or intravenous feeding need special attention to biotin intake.

VITAMIN B9
(FOLIC ACID)

It is now well established that folic acid plays a fundamental role in the prevention of neural tube defects such as spina bifida and anencephaly in developing foetuses. Known also as folate or vitamin B9, the vitamin is also necessary for healthy nervous system functioning. Like other B vitamins, folic acid aids in the formation of red blood cells, the metabolism of protein, and the synthesis of DNA and RNA. It is also important for cell division and replication. The vitamin helps manufacture white blood cells and is necessary for immune-system functioning.

Celery

· DOSAGES ·

RECOMMENDED DOSAGE Men, 200mcg; women, 200mcg; women planning a pregnancy, 400mcg. A folate supplement (400mcg) is routinely prescribed preconceptually. Pregnancy and lactation drains folate stores and so recommendations are increased to 300mcg and 260mcg respectively.

DEFICIENCY SYMPTOMS Appetite loss, diarrhoea, fatigue, insomnia, pallor, and a red, inflamed tongue. Extreme folic acid deficiency – often seen in alcoholics – can cause folic acid anaemia, characterized by malformation and reduction of red blood cells.

FOOD SOURCES Folic acid is found in a variety of foods and in a variety of forms, including green leafy vegetables, nuts, grains, and liver. Food preparation, in particular boiling, can destroy folates. Availability depends on the presence of inhibitors and other factors. For instance, the availability of folate from lettuce, eggs, oranges,and wheatgerm can be half that from lima beans, liver, yeast, and bananas.

SPECIAL NEEDS The chronic use of certain drugs used in epilepsy and inflammatory bowel disease can be associated with folate deficiency, as can intestinal malabsorption. Chronic alcoholism is the most common form of folate deficiency for a number of reasons, including poor diet. Dietary deficiency also occurs where poor diets are consistently followed, for instance in the elderly. Repeated pregnancies also increase the risk of deficiency, particularly in cases where supplements have not been taken.

CAUTIONS A toxic level of folic acid has not been established, but daily doses above 400mcg can mask symptoms of pernicious anaemia and counteract anti-epileptic drugs.

VITAMIN B12 (COBALAMIN)

Vitamin B12, also known as cobalamin, is best known for its role in preventing pernicious anaemia. Treatment involves administration of the vitamin, making sure that one other essential factor, the intrinsic factor, is also present to ensure that adequate absorption of the vitamin occurs. Intrinsic factor is normally found in gastric juice in the stomach. However, diseases affecting the stomach or surgical removal of part of the stomach may result in inadequate absorption of vitamin B12. Pernicious anaemia is a nutritional disease that can damage the nervous system if not treated. Vitamin B12 also works with folic acid to regulate the formation of red blood cells and deficiency of both vitamins results in the development of megalobastic anaemia. Just like other B vitamins, B12 helps in the metabolism of carbohydrate, fats, and protein, and has an essential role in the maintenance of the nervous system.

Dried seaweed

· DOSAGES ·

RECOMMENDED DOSAGE Adults, 1.5mcg/day; pregnant women, 1.5mcg/day; lactating women, 2.0mcg/day. Pregnant and breastfeeding women are advised to increase their intake of vitamin B12 in order to ensure that adequate amounts are present in the diet to meet the increased needs.

DEFICIENCY SYMPTOMS Typical symptoms of deficiency include weakness, a sore tongue, and diarrhoea. However, vitamin B12 deficiency usually occurs as a result of gastrointestinal disease.

FOOD SOURCES The amount of vitamin B12 in the diet varies with the amount of dietary protein. Food sources include Brewer's yeast, dairy products, meat, fish, and seaweed.

SPECIAL NEEDS Because dietary vitamin B12 is exclusively of animal origin, strict vegetarians and vegans who eat no dairy products in their diet are at risk of deficiency. Vegans should be advised to include a multivitamin supplement containing vitamin B12 on a daily basis. Others at risk include people with gastrointestinal problems, people on certain drugs and with certain congenital disorders. For specific advise about your particular situation you should consult your doctor.

ACNE

SYMPTOMS Acne is an inflammatory skin disorder. It occurs when hormones stimulate the overproduction of keratin and sebum, which in turn get caught in the skin's pores, causing blackheads. Often bacteria mixes with the excess keratin and sebum, resulting in infected whiteheads and cyst-like pustules. While acne generally affects the face, it also occurs on the neck, chest, and back, and can be mild to severe.

HOW VITAMIN B5 AND VITAMIN B6 CAN HELP The family of B vitamins play an essential role in maintaining healthy skin and helping to protect and fight infection.

DOSAGES For information about the recommended dosage for individual vitamins refer to each specific vitamin listed. However, you would be best advised to take a multivitamin that contains the recommended dosage for each of the vitamins. Always consult your doctor about the appropriate treatment and dosage of vitamin supplement. For further advice on the dosage consult your pharmacist.

· TOPICAL CREAM ·

Topical creams are a popular treatment for acne. These products usually contain ingredients such as glycolic acid, salicylic acid, sulphur, or benzoyl peroxide. Recent studies, however, have found certain B vitamins may also be effective when used topically to fight pimples. In one trial, acne patients used a cream containing 20 per cent vitamin B5, applying it from four to six times a day. Test subjects with moderate acne saw improvements within two months; individuals with severe acne saw improvement after six months. Niacin, also known as vitamin B3, is another B-complex vitamin that may help people with acne.

ASTHMA

SYMPTOMS Asthma is an inflammation of the airways caused by an allergic reaction. Although not all sufferers are allergic to the same substances, some common triggers are animal hairs, dust mites, mould spores, and pollen. When a trigger is inhaled, the body's antibodies react with the allergen, producing allergen-suppressing histamine and other chemicals. Also, chest muscles constrict, the bronchial lining swells, and the body creates more mucus, thus causing difficulty breathing, coughing (sometimes accompanied by mucus), painless tightness in the chest, and wheezing.

HOW VITAMIN B6 CAN HELP B vitamins are essential water-soluble vitamins that the body is unable to store in any significant amount. It is therefore important to ensure that you have an adequate intake of these vitamins to maintain good health and also to help to minimize the risk of complications like infection, particularly if you are susceptible to conditions such as asthma.

DOSAGES For information about the recommended dosage for individual vitamins refer to each specific vitamin listed. However, you would be best advised to take a multivitamin that contains the recommended dosage for each of the vitamins. Always consult your doctor about the appropriate treatment and dosage of vitamin supplement. For further advice on the dosage consult your pharmacist.

· ASTHMATIC SUFFERERS ·

Most studies show that the prevalence of asthma in the UK has increased. Currently, over 3.4 million people in the UK suffer with asthmatic symptoms. This includes one in seven children (aged 2–15 years) who are receiving treatment and one in 25 adults. Some researchers estimate that 20 per cent of people with asthma can be described as having a severe condition. This means that they may have daily symptoms. The Global Initiative for Asthma currently estimates that 150 million people worldwide have asthma and that the UK has the highest rates of asthma for young adults in Europe. Deaths from asthma peaked in the late 1980s and 39 deaths per million of the UK population. Since then there has been a gradual decline in deaths but the overall costs are a significant burden to the Health Service. There are additional costs in terms of absence from work and lost productivity, as well as sickness and invalidity benefits. However, the biggest burden is to the people who suffer with asthma and the reduction in their quality of life.

CANKER SORES

SYMPTOMS It is not known exactly what causes canker sores, or aphthous ulcers, as they are also known – though irritation from dental work, nutritional deficiencies, a poorly functioning immune system, and stress have all been implicated. These small, painful ulcers can appear singly or in clusters on the gums, insides of the cheeks, insides of the lips, or on the tongue. Each ulcer contains a coagulated mixture of fluid, bacteria, and white blood cells.

HOW VITAMIN B1, VITAMIN B2, AND VITAMIN B6 CAN HELP

Deficiency of the B-complex vitamins is usually depicted by mouth sores and lesions around the mouth and tongue as the vitamins are responsible for maintaining healthy tissue and protecting mucous membranes. However, if you have a recurrent problem with mouth sores you should consult your doctor for specific advice and treatment for your particular symptoms.

DOSAGES For information about the recommended dosage for individual vitamins refer to each specific vitamin listed. However, you would be best advised to take a multivitamin that contains the recommended dosage for each of the vitamins. Always consult your doctor about the appropriate treatment and dosage of vitamin supplement. For further advice on the dosage consult your pharmacist.

GINGIVITIS

SYMPTOMS Caused by deposits of plaque along the gum line, gingivitis is a painless condition characterized by swollen, soft, red gums that bleed easily during brushing and flossing. If left untreated, gingivitis can worsen into periodontitis and tooth loss.

HOW VITAMIN B9 CAN HELP The B vitamins cannot cure gingivitis – only professional dental treatment and regular brushing and flossing, in line with good oral hygiene, can do that. However, making sure that you have a healthy diet with an adequate intake of nutrients including the B vitamins will help you maintain healthy teeth and gums. For specific advice about gingivitis consult your dentist or local oral hygienist.

DOSAGES For information about the recommended dosage for individual vitamins refer to each specific vitamin listed. However, you would be best advised to take a multivitamin that contains the recommended dosage for each of the vitamins. Always consult your doctor about the appropriate treatment and dosage of vitamin supplement. For further advice on the dosage consult your pharmacist.

CARPAL TUNNEL SYNDROME

SYMPTOMS The carpal tunnel is a passageway through the wrist that protects those nerves and tendons that link the arm and hand. When the tissue that constitutes the tunnel becomes inflamed through repetitive motion, carpal tunnel syndrome occurs. The result is numbness or tingling in the hand and fingers and pain in the wrist that may shoot up into the forearm or down into the fingers.

HOW VITAMIN B6 CAN HELP The B vitamins cannot cure carpal tunnel syndrome but together with a healthy diet they can help to make sure that tissues are maintained in a way that minimizes the risk of damage and maximizes the potential for repair. If you have a problem with tingling hands and fingers you should consult your doctor for advice and treatment for your particular symptoms.

DOSAGES For information about the recommended dosage for individual vitamins refer to each specific vitamin listed. However, you would be best advised to take a multivitamin that contains the recommended dosage for each of the vitamins. For further advice on the dosage consult your pharmacist.

· INFLAMED JOINTS ·

A bursa is a sac-like membrane that acts as a cushion between the bone and fibrous tissues of the muscles and tendons. Its job is to facilitate movement by limiting friction. When a bursa becomes inflamed through repeated physical activity, the result is bursitis. Symptoms include pain and swelling in a joint, usually the elbow, hip, knee, shoulder, or big toe. Vitamin B12 and vitamin B3 may help to relieve bursitis symptoms, although consult your doctor first for advice and treatment for your particular symptoms.

OSTEOARTHRITIS

SYMPTOMS Osteoarthritis, also known simply as arthritis, is one of the most common disorders known to humans, affecting up to 80 per cent of all individuals over the age of 60. Caused by simple wear and tear on a joint, arthritis is considered a degenerative disease. Symptoms include mild to moderately severe pain in a joint during or after use, discomfort in a joint during a weather change, swelling in an affected joint, and loss of flexibility in an affected joint.

HOW VITAMIN B3 CAN HELP Together with a healthy diet, the B vitamins can help to maintain healthy joint tissue and circulating fluids.

DOSAGES Osteoarthritis is a serious condition that requires medical treatment. You should consult your doctor first for advice and treatment for your particular symptoms. For information about the recommended dosage for individual vitamins refer to each specific vitamin listed. However, you would be best advised to take a multivitamin that contains the recommended dosage for each of the vitamins. For further advice on the dosage consult your pharmacist.

· FOLIC ACID AND NEURAL TUBE DEFECTS ·

Pregnancy is not the time to begin experimenting with large doses of different vitamins. It is imperative, however, that you get enough nutrients during this time to support a quickly-developing foetus. One of the most talked-about vitamins for foetal development is folic acid, also called vitamin B9 and folate, which is famous for its role in the development of genetic material such as RNA and DNA. Because nearly half of pregnancies are unplanned, it is important for women to get enough folic acid throughout their childbearing years – thus ensuring that any unintentional pregnancy will be a healthy one. Here's how the vitamin can help:

◆ Deficiencies of folic acid have been linked in studies to low birth weight in infants. In one study, folic acid supplements in pregnant women improved birth weight and decreased the incidence of foetal growth retardation and maternal infections.

◆ Research has linked low folic acid intake to neural tube defects such as spina bifida. Women have been reported to lower their risk of having a child with spina bifida by 75 per cent if they take folic acid supplements prior to and during pregnancy.

DIABETES

SYMPTOMS To understand diabetes, it helps to know something about the pancreas. The organ – long, thin, and situated behind the stomach – is responsible for regulating the body's use of glucose. To do so, the pancreas creates a number of chemicals, including insulin. When blood glucose levels begin to rise, it is insulin's job to prod muscle and fat cells to absorb whatever glucose they need for future activities; the liver stores any surplus. Some individuals, however, either do not produce enough insulin or their body resists whatever insulin is produced, thus necessitating an outside source is required. Either way, the result is the same: diabetes – specifically, diabetes Type 1 and diabetes Type 2.

Both Type 1 and Type 2 have a genetic basis. Type 1 usually affects children and young adults. Type 2, or maturity-onset diabetes, usually occurs in adults aged over 40 and is linked to obesity. The classic symptoms of untreated diabetes include excessive thirst, extreme tiredness, increased urination, blurred vision and itching skin, particularly around the genital organs. If not treated, diabetes can cause serious complications, namely heart disease, kidney damage, blindness, stroke, and nerve damage, which can result in foot and leg amputations.

HOW VITAMIN B7 AND VITAMIN B12 CAN HELP It is important for people with diabetes to eat a balanced diet and make sure that they have an adequate intake of all nutrients including B vitamins. However, it is the case that because people with diabetes tend to excrete more vitamin B2 or Riboflavin they may have increased needs for this vitamin.

DOSAGES For information about the recommended dosage for individual vitamins refer to each specific vitamin listed. However, you would be best advised to take a multivitamin that contains the recommended dosage for each of the vitamins. Always consult your doctor about the appropriate treatment and dosage of vitamin supplement. For further advice on the dosage consult your pharmacist.

· EAT YOUR WAY TO HEALTH ·

When you have diabetes it is important to have regular check-ups with your local diabetes healthcare team. Diet is important, whether you have Type 1 or Type 2 diabetes. However, you do not have to eat special diabetic foods. The important thing is to enjoy a range of foods and base meals on starchy foods such as bread, potatoes, rice, pasta, and cereals. it is also important to eat plenty of fruit and vegetables. You should cut down on fat, particularly saturated animal fat and salt. There is no need to cut out sugar altogether but limit your intake so that you avoid sugary drinks and confectionery like boiled sweets.

DEPRESSION

SYMPTOMS The condition often begins with no apparent trigger, though it can also develop from adjustment disorder. Symptoms can include change in appetite, decreased self-esteem, grief, helplessness, impaired daily functioning, irritability, loss of interest in once enjoyable activities, inappropriate guilt, lethargy, neglect of physical appearance, malaise, self-reproach, sense of doom, sleep disturbances, slowed physical and mental responses, social withdrawal, and suicidal thoughts.

HOW VITAMIN B6 AND VITAMIN B9 CAN HELP Over the years, research has implicated various nutrients, including vitamins, and their deficiencies with depression. However, there is no conclusive evidence to suggest that B vitamins will cure your depression. Having a healthy diet and lifestyle and maintaining your weight at a reasonable level is the best way to protect yourself from depressive states.

DOSAGES For information about the recommended dosage for individual vitamins refer to each specific vitamin listed. However, you would be best advised to take a multivitamin that contains the recommended dosage for each of the vitamins. Always consult your doctor about the appropriate treatment and dosage of vitamin supplement. For further advice on the dosage consult your pharmacist.

· MIGRAINE MEDICINE ·

Also called a vascular headache, a migraine is an extremely painful headache that occurs when cerebral blood vessels constrict, allowing less blood to reach the brain. The one constant symptom is severe head pain – often so extreme that individuals become nauseated and vomit. The pain typically begins on one side of the head and may gradually spread and throb.

Migraines are usually preceded by several warning signs. Two to eight hours before the migraine occurs, there may be cravings for sweets, elation, drowsiness, intense thirst, and irritability. About 15 to 30 minutes before the migraine a group of signs occur that can include blank spots within the field of vision, dizziness, sparkling flashes of light, temporary numbness or paralysis of one side of the body, and zigzag lines that cross the field of vision. It is not known why some people get migraines, although in some individuals, stress, alcohol consumption, specific foods, and oral contraceptives can trigger the cerebral vessels to constrict, causing vascular headaches.

B vitamins are not recognized treatments for headaches and migraine but if you suffer with migraines that are related to certain foods you may be restricting your dietary intake. Therefore you need to take a multivitamin supplement to ensure that you have an adequate intake – particularly in the case of the water–soluble vitamins, which the body does not store.

FIBROCYSTIC DISEASE

SYMPTOMS Benign breast disease, chronic cystic mastitis, lumpy breasts, and mammary dysplasia are all names for fibrocystic disease, a condition characterized by one or more lumps in one or both breasts. These lumps may or may not be painful and may be accompanied by greenish or straw-coloured discharge from the nipples. Unlike malignant tumours, these benign lumps are actually cysts, fluid-filled sacs that tend to get bigger toward the end of the menstrual cycle, when the body retains more fluid. Some cysts can be tiny, others can be the size of an egg. It isn't known exactly what causes fibrocystic disease, although an imbalance of ovarian hormones are believed to play a role. The disease occurs mainly in women between the ages of 25 and 50 and usually disappears with menopause.

HOW VITAMIN B6 CAN HELP The family of B vitamins can play an essential role in helping to protect and fight infection.

DOSAGES For information about the recommended dosage for individual vitamins refer to each specific vitamin listed. However, you would be best advised to take a multivitamin that contains the recommended dosage for each of the vitamins. Always consult your doctor about the appropriate treatment and dosage of vitamin supplement. For further advice on the dosage consult your pharmacist.

· ATTENTION DEFICIT DISORDER ·

Attention deficit disorder (ADD), or attention deficit–hyperactivity disorder (ADHD) as it is also called, is a disorder that primarily affects children and is associated with learning difficulties and lack of social skills. It is defined as age-inappropriate impulsiveness, lack of concentration, and sometimes excessive physical activity. While the cause of the condition is unknown, theories include foetal exposure to alcohol, drugs, or cigarette smoke; preconception paternal recreational drug and/or alcohol use (which can affect sperm quality); allergies; or poor diet. The majority of sufferers outgrow the condition by their late teens.

Conventional treatment for ADD is Ritalin, an amphetamine-like drug which is a stimulant in adults but often has a calming effect in children with ADD. Vitamin B6 may also help to relieve the symptoms of ADD.

Note: Before giving your child vitamin B6 supplements, consult a doctor. Although the side effects from vitamin B6 supplements are rare, at very high levels this vitamin can damage sensory nerves, leading to numbness in the hands and feet as well as difficulty when walking.

CERVICAL DYSPLASIA

SYMPTOMS Cervical dysplasia is an asymptomatic condition found most often in women between the ages of 25 and 35. It has been linked to sexually transmitted diseases, such as the human papillomavirus (HPV), which causes genital warts. Infection by sexually transmitted organisms may be accompanied by oxidants, which can damage cervical cell DNA. Eventually, this cellular damage can lead to cancer.

HOW VITAMIN B9 CAN HELP The family of B vitamins can play an essential role in helping to protect and fight infection.

DOSAGES For information about the recommended dosage for individual vitamins refer to each specific vitamin listed. However, you would be best advised to take a multivitamin that contains the recommended dosage for each of the vitamins. Always consult your doctor about the appropriate treatment and dosage of vitamin supplement. For further advice on the dosage consult your pharmacist.

DYSMENORRHOEA

SYMPTOMS Mild to moderate pain during menstruation is normal and occurs when the uterus contracts to shed its temporary lining. However, sometimes the uterus contracts more than necessary, causing extreme pain. This condition is called dysmenorrhoea. It is believed to be caused by excessive levels of prostaglandins. The primary symptom is strong to severe pain in the lower abdomen during menstruation (this pain may radiate to the hips, buttocks, or thighs), nausea, vomiting, diarrhoea, and general aching. Other signs may include dizziness, excessive perspiration, and fatigue.

HOW VITAMIN B3 CAN HELP The family of B vitamins play an essential role in helping to protect and fight infection.

DOSAGES For information about the recommended dosage for individual vitamins refer to each specific vitamin listed. However, you would be best advised to take a multivitamin that contains the recommended dosage for each of the vitamins. Always consult your doctor about the appropriate treatment and dosage of vitamin supplement. For further advice on the dosage consult your pharmacist.

MENOPAUSE

SYMPTOMS Menopause is not an illness but a natural condition that occurs when the ovaries no longer produce enough oestrogen to stimulate the lining of the uterus and vagina properly. Simply put, menopause is when women no longer menstruate or get pregnant. It generally occurs somewhere between the ages of 40 and 60. One of the most famous signs of menopause is the hot flush, a sudden reddening of the face accompanied by a feeling of intense warmth. Other common symptoms include depressed mood, fluid retention, headache, insomnia, irritability, nervousness, night sweats, painful intercourse, rapid heartbeat, susceptibility to bladder problems, thinning of vaginal tissues, vaginal dryness, and weight gain. It should be noted that some women experience few symptoms, while still others encounter none at all.

HOW VITAMIN B6 AND VITAMIN B9 CAN HELP The B-complex vitamins target heart disease and stroke, two illnesses that are prevalent among menopausal women. Research has shown that in menopausal women, both vitamin B6 (pyridoxine) and vitamin B9 (folic acid) reduce body levels of homocysteine, a naturally occurring amino acid that has been implicated in coronary artery disease and stroke.

DOSAGES For information about the recommended dosage for individual vitamins refer to each specific vitamin listed. However, you would be best advised to take a multivitamin that contains the recommended dosage for each of the vitamins. Always consult your doctor about the appropriate treatment and dosage of vitamin supplement. For further advice on the dosage consult your pharmacist.

PREMENSTRUAL SYNDROME

SYMPTOMS Premenstrual syndrome, popularly known as PMS, is a predictable pattern of physical and emotional changes that occurs in some women just before menstruation. Symptoms range from barely noticeable to extreme and can include abdominal swelling, anxiety, bloating, breast soreness, clumsiness, depressed mood, difficulty concentrating, fatigue, fluid retention, headaches, irritability, lethargy, skin eruptions, sleep disturbances, swollen hands and feet, and weight gain. While it is not known exactly what causes the condition, theories include hormonal, nutritional, and psychological factors.

HOW VITAMIN B6 CAN HELP Oral doses of vitamin B6 or pyridoxine have been used to treat PMS and some women seem to gain some relief from symptoms when taking the vitamin. However, some severe toxicity has resulted from the use of pyridoxine in PMS treatment and so some degree of caution is necessary when using this treatment. Severe sensory neuropathy of hands and feet may develop with chronic doses of 100–200mg per day.

Contraceptive agents do not increase pyridoxine requirements but large doses may suppress some of the symptoms that can manifest themselves when using oral contraceptives.

DOSAGES For information about the recommended dosage for individual vitamins refer to each specific vitamin listed. However, you would be best advised to take a multivitamin that contains the recommended dosage for each of the vitamins. Always consult your doctor about the appropriate treatment and dosage of vitamin supplement.

ALTERNATIVE HEALTH STRATEGIES

Herbs, vitamins, and minerals all contribute to good health. However, creating a sense of general well-being involves more than simply taking supplements. Health has to do with a quality of life that can often be aggravated by causes of harmful stress. Listed below are some additional ways to help keep yourself well.

IMPROVE YOUR EATING HABITS

Here are the five main eating strategies people follow; consider finding the healthiest one that works with your lifestyle.

- Omnivore
- Semi-vegetarian
- Macrobiotic
- Vegan
- Vegetarian

Legumes

GET MORE EXERCISE

Whether it's walking or weightlifting, any type of exercise can help you feel better. Try any of these types:

- Stretching
- Aerobics
- Resistance training

Exercise by walking as much as possible.

SIMPLE WAYS TO EASE STRESS

In addition to exercise and healthy eating, here are some more techniques – old and new – for easing stress and increasing relaxation.

- Get enough sleep
- Take time to relax
- Give up junk food
- Adopt a pet
- Surround yourself with supportive people
- Limit your exposure to chemicals
- Enjoy yourself

· ONE-MINUTE STRESS REDUCER ·

Deep breathing can be done anywhere and anytime you need to calm and centre yourself:

1 Inhale deeply through your nose.
2 Hold your breath for up to three seconds, then exhale your breath through your mouth.
3 Continue as needed.

Deep breathing draws a person's attention away from a given stress and refocuses it on his or her breathing. This type of breathing is not only comforting (thanks to its rhythmic quality), but also has been shown to lower rapid pulse and shallow respiration – two temporary symptoms of stress.

GET MOVING

Ask medical experts to name one stay-young strategy and there's a good chance that "exercise" will be the answer. And with good reason. Exercise, whether a gentle walk around the block or a full-tilt weight lifting session, strengthens the heart, lowers the body's resting heart rate, builds muscles, boosts circulation to the body and the brain, revs up the metabolism and burns calories. All of which can keep a person looking and feeling his or her best. For it to be effective, exercise several times a week. Aim for at least three sessions. For optimum health, try a combination of aerobic exercise and strength training. And don't forget to stretch before and after each workout!

Cycling

STRETCHING

WHAT IT IS Any movement that stretches muscles. Examples include bending at the waist and touching the toes, sitting with legs outstretched in front of you, and rolling your neck. Stretch for eight to 12 minutes before every workout and again after you exercise.

WHY IT'S IMPORTANT Muscles act like springs. If a muscle is short and tight, it loses the ability to absorb shock. The less shock a muscle can absorb, the more strain there is on the joints. Thus, stretching maintains flexibility, which in turn prevents injuries. Because we often lose our regular range of motion with age, stretching is especially important for older adults to prevent sprains, strains and falls.

POPULAR EATING STRATEGIES

Full stretch

Leg tuck

Stretch regularly to maintain flexibility.

AEROBICS

WHAT IT IS Any activity that uses large muscle groups, is maintained continuously for 15 minutes or more, and is rhythmic in nature. Examples include aerobic dance, jogging, skating and walking. Ideally, you should aim for three to six aerobic workouts per week.

WHY IT'S IMPORTANT Aerobic exercise trains the heart, lungs, and cardiovascular system to process and deliver oxygen more quickly and efficiently to every part of the body. As the heart muscle becomes stronger and more efficient, a larger amount of blood can be pumped with each stroke. Fewer strokes are then required to rapidly transport oxygen to all parts of the body.

Aerobic exercise

RESISTANCE TRAINING

WHAT IT IS Any activity that improves the condition of your muscles by making repeated movements against a force. Examples include lifting large or small weights, sit-ups, stair-stepping, and isometrics.

WHY IT'S IMPORTANT Resistance training makes it easier to move heavy loads, whether they require carrying, pushing, pulling, or lifting, as well as participating in sports that require strength. The exercises are of various kinds. Some require changing the length of the muscle while maintaining the level of tension, others involve using special equipment to vary the tension in the muscles, and some entail contracting a muscle while maintaining its length.

Press-up

POPULAR EATING STRATEGIES

EATING SMART

A balanced diet is the foundation of good health. For proof, just read the numerous medical studies that link healthy eating with disease prevention and disease reversal. These same studies connect high fat intake, high sodium consumption, and diets with too much protein to numerous illnesses, including cancer, cardiovascular diseases, diverticular diseases, hypertension, and heart disease. But what exactly is a balanced diet? Generally speaking, it is a diet comprised of carbohydrates, dietary fibre, fat, protein, water, 13 vitamins and 20 minerals. More specifically, it is a diet built around a wide variety of fruits, legumes, whole grains, and vegetables. Alcohol, animal protein, high-fat foods, high-sodium foods, highly-sugared foods, fizzy drinks, and processed foods are consumed sparingly.

Citrus fruits

OMNIVOROUS

ON THE MENU Plant-based foods, dairy products, eggs, fish, seafood, red meats, organ meats, poultry.

FOODS THAT ARE AVOIDED None. Everything is fair game.

Egg

HOW HEALTHY IS IT? It depends. Someone who eats eggs, poultry, or meat every day, chooses refined snacks over whole foods, and gets only one or two daily servings of fruits and vegetables will not be as healthy as a person who limits meat (the general dietary term for any "flesh foods", including poultry and fish) to two or three times a week, chooses water over soft drinks, and gets the recommended five or more daily servings of fruits and vegetables. Complaints about traditional omnivorous diets revolve around the diet's high levels of cholesterol and saturated fat (found in animal-based foods), which increase the risk of cancer, diabetes, heart disease, and obesity. However, an omnivorous diet can be healthful one provided thoughtful choices are made. To keep cholesterol and saturated fat to a minimum and nutrients to a maximum, eat five or more daily servings of fruits and vegetables, choose whole grains over refined grains, enjoy daily legume or soyfood protein sources, and limit the use of animal foods.

Watercress

MACROBIOTIC

ON THE MENU Plant-based foods, fish, very limited amounts of salt.

FOODS THAT ARE AVOIDED Dairy products, eggs, foods with artificial ingredients, hot spices, mass-produced foods, organ meats, peppers, potatoes, poultry, red meats, shellfish, warm drinks, and refined foods.

HOW HEALTHY IS IT? Macrobiotics is based on a system created in the early 1900s by Japanese philosopher George Ohsawa. The diet consists of 50 per cent whole grains, 20-30 per cent vegetables, and 5-10 per cent beans, sea vegetables, and soy foods. The remainder of the diet is composed of white-meat fish, fruits, and nuts. The diet's low amounts of saturated fat, absence of processed foods, and emphasis on high-fibre foods such as whole grains and vegetables, may promote cardiovascular health. Because soy and sea vegetables contain cancer-fighting compounds, a macrobiotic diet is often recommended to help treat cancer. However, critics worry that the diet's limited variety of food can leave followers lacking in certain vitamins and important cancer-fighting phytonutrients.

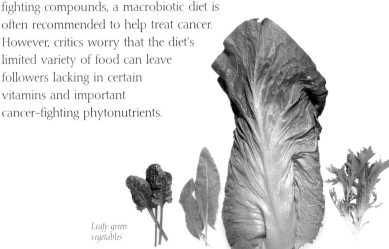

Leafy green vegetables

SEMI-VEGETARIAN

ON THE MENU Plant-based foods, dairy products, eggs, fish, seafood.

FOODS THAT ARE AVOIDED Red meats, organ meats, poultry.

HOW HEALTHY IS IT? Like an omnivorous diet, a semi-vegetarian diet is as healthy as a person makes it. Individuals who eat high-fat and highly processed foods fail to get the recommended daily number of vegetables and fruits, and eschew whole grains for processed grains will not enjoy optimum health. That said, individuals who are conscientious about eating a balanced, varied diet, and who limit fish and seafood intake to two or three times per week, can expect a lower risk of heart disease. Since many oily fish contain omega-3 fatty acids, eating them in moderation has been found to help lower blood cholesterol. Be aware, however, that oily saltwater fish such as shark, swordfish and tuna have been found to carry mercury in their tissues; many health authorities recommend eating these varieties no more than once or twice a week. Also, due to overfishing, many fish species are now threatened, including bluefin tuna, Pacific perch, Chilean sea bass, Chinook salmon, and swordfish.

Shellfish

VEGAN

ON THE MENU Plant-based foods.

FOODS THAT ARE AVOIDED Dairy, eggs, fish, seafood, red meats, organ meats, poultry. Also avoided are foods made by animals or processed with animal parts, such as gelatin, honey, marshmallows made with animal gelatin, white sugar processed with bone char.

HOW HEALTHY IS IT? A vegan (pronounced VEE–gun) diet can be extremely healthful. Like the vegetarian diet, a vegan diet has been shown by numerous studies to lower blood pressure and prevent heart disease. In addition, the high fibre intake cuts the risk of diverticular disease and colon cancer. Yet because vegans do not eat dairy products or eggs, they must be more conscientious than vegetarians about eating plant foods with vitamin B12 and vitamin D or taking supplements of these nutrients.

Lettuce

VEGETARIAN

ON THE MENU Plant-based foods, dairy, eggs.

FOODS THAT ARE AVOIDED Fish, gelatin, seafood, red meats, organ meats, poultry.

HOW HEALTHY IS IT? A vegetarian diet can be very healthy when done right. Fortunately, this isn't hard. Dietary science has debunked theories of "protein combining" popular in the 1960s and 1970s, leaving today's vegetarians to worry only about eating a wide variety of whole foods including beans, fruits, grains, low-fat dairy products, nuts, soy foods, and vegetables. A varied daily diet insures enough protein, calcium, and other nutrients for vegetarians of all ages, including children, pregnant individuals, and the elderly. A well-chosen vegetarian eating plan has been shown by numerous studies to lower blood pressure, decrease the risk of breast cancer, and prevent heart disease. In addition, the diet's high fibre levels cut the risk of diverticular disease and colon cancer.

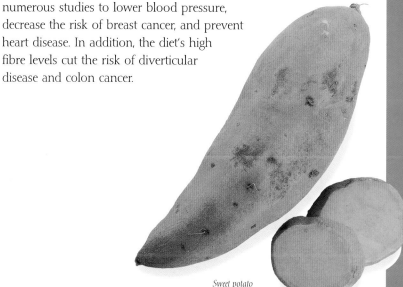

Sweet potato

NUTRIENT KNOW-HOW

Vitamins and minerals are known collectively as nutrients. Name a body function such as carbohydrate metabolism, nerve cell replication, or wound healing and you'll find one or more of these nutrients at work. The best place to look for vitamins and minerals? In the food you eat every day. Indeed, if you eat a well-balanced diet

there is a good chance you'll get all the nutrients your body needs. But if you are ill, pregnant, eat an inadequate diet, drink more than two alcoholic or caffeinated drinks per day, are under stress, are taking certain medications, or have difficulty absorbing certain nutrients, you may need to supplement your diet with one or more vitamins or minerals. Supplements generally come in tablet and capsule form, although some health food stores also carry liquid supplements. Whichever form you choose, doses are measured by weight in milligrams (mg); in micrograms (mcg); or in the universal standard known as international units (IU).

VITAMIN A
(beta carotene, retinol)

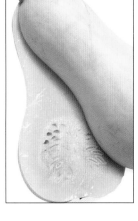

What It Does Vitamin A is found in two forms: performed vitamin A, known as retinol, and provitamin A, called beta carotene. Retinol is found only in foods of animal origin. Beta carotene, a carotenoid, is a pigment found in plants. Beta carotene has a slight nutritional edge, boasting antioxidant properties and the ability to help lower harmful cholesterol levels. Regardless of the form, vitamin A is essential for good vision, promotes healthy skin, hair, and mucous membranes, stimulates wound healing, and is necessary for the proper development of bones and teeth.

EU Recommended Daily Allowance 800μg.
Food Sources: Orange and yellow fruits and vegetables, dark green leafy vegetables, whole milk, cream, butter, organ meats.

Toxic Dosage When taken excessively vitamin A can cause abdominal pain, amenorrhoea, dry skin, enlarged liver or spleen, hair loss, headaches, itching, joint pain, nausea, vision problems, vomiting.

Enemies Antibiotics, cholesterol-lowering drugs, heavy laxative use.

Deficiency Symptoms Because vitamin A is fat-soluble, it is stored in the body's fat for a long time, making deficiency uncommon. However, deficiency symptoms include dryness of the conjunctiva and cornea, frequent colds, insomnia, night blindness, reproductive difficulties, and respiratory infections.

VITAMIN B$_1$
(thiamine)

What It Does Maintains normal nervous system functioning, helps metabolize carbohydrates, proteins, and fats; assists in blood formation and circulation; optimizes cognitive activity and brain function; regulates the body's appetite; protects the body from the degenerative effects of alcohol consumption, environmental pollution, and smoking.

Minimum Recommended Daily Allowance 1.4mg.

Food Sources Brewer's yeast, broccoli, brown rice, egg yolks, fish, legumes, peanuts, peas, pork, prunes, oatmeal, raisins, rice bran, soybeans, wheatgerm, whole grains.

Toxic Dosage There is no know toxicity level for vitamin B1.
Enemies: Antibiotics, a diet high in simple carbohydrates, heavy physical exertion, oral contraceptives.

Deficiency Symptoms Appetite loss, confusion, fatigue, heart arrhythmia, nausea, mood swings. Severe deficiency can lead to beriberi, a crippling disease characterized by convulsions, diarrhoea, edema, gastrointestinal problems, heart failure, mental confusion, nerve damage, paralysis, and severe weight loss.

VITAMIN B₂
(riboflavin, vitamin G)

What It Does Helps metabolize carbohydrates, fats, and proteins; allows skin, nail, and hair tissues to utilize oxygen; aids in red blood cell formation and antibody production; promotes cell respiration; maintains proper nerve function, eyes, and adrenal glands.

Minimum Recommended Daily Allowance 1.6mg.

Food Sources Cheese, egg yolks, fish, legumes, milk, poultry, spinach, whole grains, yoghurt.

Toxic Dosage There is no known toxicity level for this vitamin, although nervousness and rapid heartbeat have been reported with daily dosages of 10mg.

Enemies Alcohol, oral contraceptives, strenuous exercise.

Deficiency Symptoms Cracks at the corners of the mouth, dermatitis, dizziness, hair loss, insomnia, itchy or burning eyes, light sensitivity, mouth sores, impaired thinking, inflammation of the tongue, rashes.

VITAMIN B₅
(pantothenic acid)

What It Does Helps produce adrenal hormones, antibodies, and various neurotransmitters; reduces skin inflammation; speeds healing of wounds; helps convert food to energy.

Minimum Recommended Daily Allowance 6mg.

Food Sources Beef, eggs, beans, brown rice, corn, lentils, mushrooms, nuts, peas, pork, saltwater fish, sweet potatoes.

Toxic Dosages There is no known toxicity level for this vitamin; however, doses above 10mg can cause diarrhoea in some individuals.

Deficiency Symptoms Vitamin B5 deficiency is extremely rare and is likely to occur only with starvation.

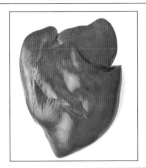

VITAMIN B₆
(pyridoxine)

What It Does Involved in more bodily functions than nearly any other nutrient. It helps the body metabolize carbohydrates, fats and proteins; supports immune function; helps build red blood cells; assists in transmission of nerve impulses; maintains the body's sodium and potassium balance; helps synthesize RNA and DNA.

Minimum Recommended Daily Allowance 2mg.

Food Sources Avocados, bananas, beans, blackstrap molasses, brown rice, carrots, corn, fish, nuts, sunflower seeds.

Toxic Dosage Levels of over 500mg can cause numbness in the hands and feet.

Deficiency Symptoms Vitamin B6 deficiency is rare. Symptoms include depression, fatigue, flaky skin, headaches, insomnia, irritability, muscle weakness, nausea.

VITAMIN B₁₂
(cobalamin)

What It Does Regulates formation of red blood cells, helps the body utilize iron; converts carbohydrates, fats, and proteins into energy; aids in cellular formation and cellular longevity; prevents nerve damage; maintains fertility; promotes normal growth.

Minimum Recommended Daily Allowance 1μg.

Food Sources Brewer's yeast, dairy products, eggs, organ meats, seafood, sea vegetables.

Toxic Dosage There is no known toxicity level for vitamin B12.

Enemies Anti-coagulant drugs, anti-gout medication, potassium supplements.

Deficiency Symptoms While deficiency is rare, individuals who do not eat animal products are at risk unless they fortify their diets with plant-sources such as brewer's yeast and sea vegetables. Symptoms include back pain, body odour, constipation, dizziness, fatigue, moodiness, numbness and tingling in the arms and legs, ringing in the ears, muscle weakness, tongue inflammation, weight loss. Severe deficiency can lead to pernicious anaemia, characterized by abdominal pain, stiffness in the arms and legs, a tendency to bleed, yellowish cast to the skin, permanent nerve damage, death.

VITAMIN C
(ascorbic acid)

What It Does Protects against pollution and infection, enhances immunity; aids in growth and repair of both bone and tissue by helping the body produce collagen; maintains adrenal gland function; helps the body absorb iron; aids in production of anti-stress hormones; reduces cholesterol levels; lowers high blood pressure; prevents artherosclerosis.

Minimum Recommended Daily Allowance 60mg.

Food Sources Berries, cantaloupe, citrus fruits, broccoli, leafy greens, mangoes, papayas, peppers, persimmons, pineapple, tomatoes.

Toxic Dosage Doses larger than 10,000mg can cause diarrhoea, stomach irritation, or increased kidney stone formation.

Enemies Alcohol, analgesics, antidepressants, anticoagulants, oral contraceptives, smoking, steroids.

Deficiency Symptoms Bleeding gums, easy bruising, fatigue, reduced resistance to colds and other infections, slow healing of wounds, weight loss. Severe deficiency can lead to scurvy, a sometimes-fatal disease characterized by aching bones, muscle weakness, and swollen and bleeding gums.

VITAMIN D
(calciferol, ergosterol)

What It Does Helps the body utilize calcium and phosphorus; promotes normal development of bones and teeth; assists in thyroid function; maintains normal blood clotting; helps regulate heartbeat, nerve function, and muscle contraction.
Minimum Recommended Daily Allowance 5μg
Food Sources Dandelion greens, dairy products, eggs, fatty saltwater fish, parsley, sweet potatoes, vegetable oils.
Toxic Dosage Daily doses higher than 20μg can lead to raised blood calcium levels and calcium deposits of the heart, liver, and kidney.
Enemies Antacids, cholesterol-lowering drugs, cortisone drugs.
Deficiency Symptoms The body naturally manufactures about 200 IU of vitamin D when exposed to ten minutes of ultraviolet light, making deficiency rare. Symptoms include bone weakening, diarrhoea, insomnia, muscle twitches, vision disturbances. Severe deficiency can lead to rickets, a disease that results in bone defects such as bowlegs and knock-knees.

VITAMIN E
(tocopherol)

What It Does Prevents unstable molecules known as free radicals from damaging cells and tissue; accelerates wound healing; protects lung tissue from inhaled pollutants; aids in functioning of the immune system; endocrine system, and sex glands; improves circulation; promotes normal blood clotting.
Minimum Recommended Daily Allowance 10mg
Food Sources Avocados, dark green leafy vegetables, eggs, legumes, nuts, organ meats, seafood, seeds, soybeans.
Toxic Dosage Although there is no established toxicity level of vitamin E, the vitamin has blood-thinning properties; individuals who are taking anticoagulant medications or have clotting deficiencies should avoid vitamin E at doses higher than 800mg.
Enemies High temperatures and overcooking reduce vitamin E levels in food.
Deficiency Symptoms Vitamin E deficiency is rare. Deficiency symptoms include fluid retention, infertility, miscarriage, muscle degeneration.

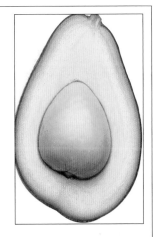

CALCIUM

What It Does Necessary for the growth and maintenance of bones, teeth, and healthy gums; maintains normal blood pressure normal; may reduce risk of heart disease; enables muscles, including the heart, to contract; is essential for normal blood clotting; needed for proper nerve impulse transmission; maintains connective tissue; helps prevent rickets and osteoporosis.

Minimum Recommended Daily Allowance 800mg.

Food Sources Asparagus, cruciferous vegetables, dairy products, dark leafy vegetables, figs, legumes, nuts, oats, prunes, salmon with bones, sardines with bones, seeds, soybeans, tofu.

Toxic Dosage Daily intake of 2,000mg or more can lead to constipation, calcium deposits in the soft tissue, urinary tract infections, and possible interference with the body's absorption of zinc.

Enemies Alcohol, caffeine, excessive sugar intake, high-protein diet, high sodium intake, inadequate levels of vitamin D, soft drinks containing phosphorous.

Deficiency Symptoms Aching joints, brittle nails, eczema, elevated blood cholesterol, heart palpitations, hypertension, insomnia, muscle cramps, nervousness, pallor, tooth decay.

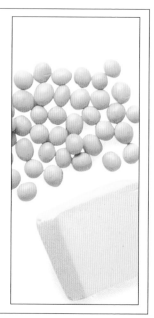

IRON

What It Does Aids in the production of haemoglobin (the protein in red blood cells that transports oxygen from the lungs to the body's tissue) and myoglobin (a protein that provides extra fuel to muscles during exertion); helps maintain healthy immune system; is important for growth.

Minimum Recommended Daily Allowance 14mg.

Food Sources Beef, blackstrap molasses, brewer's yeast, dark green vegetables, dried fruit, legumes, nuts, organ meats, sea vegetables, seeds, soybeans, whole grains.

Toxic Dosage Iron should not be taken in excess of 35mg daily without a doctor's recommendation. In high doses, iron can cause diarrhoea, dizziness, fatigue, headaches, stomach-aches, weakened pulse. Excess iron inhibits the absorption of phosphorus and vitamin E, interferes with immune function, and has been associated with cancer, cirrhosis, heart disease.

Enemies Antacids, caffeine, tetracycline, iron absorption, excessive menstrual bleeding, long-term illness, an ulcer.

Deficiency Symptoms Anaemia, brittle hair, difficulty swallowing, dizziness, fatigue, hair loss, irritability, nervousness, pallor, ridges on the nails, sensitivity to cold, slowed mental reactions.

MAGNESIUM

What It Does Plays a role in formation of bone; protects arterial linings from stress caused by sudden blood pressure; helps body metabolize carbohydrates and minerals; assists in building proteins; helps maintain healthy bones and teeth; reduces the risk of developing osteoporosis.
Minimum Recommended Daily Allowance 300mg.
Food Sources Apples, apricots, avocados, bananas, blackstrap molasses, brewer's yeast. brown rice, cantaloupe, dairy products, figs, garlic, green leafy vegetables, legumes, nuts.
Toxic Dosage Daily doses over 3,000mg can lead to diarrhoea, fatigue, muscle weakness, and in extreme cases, severely depressed heart rate and blood pressure, shallow breathing, loss of reflexes and coma.
Enemies Alcohol, diuretics, high-fat intake, high-protein diet.
Deficiency Symptoms Though deficiency is rare, symptoms include disorientation, heart palpitations, listlessness, muscle weakness.

POTASSIUM

What It Does Maintains a healthy nervous system and regular heart rhythm; helps prevent stroke; aids in proper muscle contractions; controls the body's water balance; assists chemical reactions within cells; aids in the transmission of electrochemical impulses; maintains stable blood pressure; required for protein synthesis, carbohydrate metabolism, and insulin secretion by the pancreas.
No EU Recommended Daily Allowance
Food Sources Apricots, avocados, bananas, blackstrap molasses, brewer's yeast, brown rice, citrus fruits, dairy.
Toxic Dosage Should not be taken in excess of 18 grams.
Enemies Diarrhoea, diuretics, caffeine use, heavy perspiration, kidney disorders, tobacco use.
Deficiency Symptoms Chills, dry skin, constipation, depression, diminished reflexes, edema, headaches, insatiable thirst, fluctuations in heartbeat, nervousness, respiratory distress.

ZINC

What It Does Contributes to a wide range of bodily processes. Aids in cell respiration; assists in bone development; helps energy metabolism, promotes wound healing; regulates heart rate and blood pressure; helps liver remove toxic substances, such as alcohol, from the body.
Minimum Recommended Daily Allowance 15mg
Food Sources Brewer's yeast, cheese, egg yolks, lamb, legumes, mushrooms, nuts, organ meats, sea food, sea vegetables, seeds.
Toxic Dosage Do not take more than 50mg zinc daily. In doses higher than this zinc can depress the immune system.
Deficiency Symptoms Appetite loss, dermatitis, fatigue, impaired wound healing, loss of taste, white streaks on the nails.

INDEX

ACKNOWLEDGEMENTS

DORLING KINDERSLEY

LONDON, NEW YORK, SYDNEY, DEHLI, PARIS,
MUNICH, and JOHANNESBURG

Stephanie Pedersen is an American writer and editor who specializes in the
area of health. Her articles have appeared in numerous publications and she
has also co-written several books published by St. Martin's Press.

The publisher would like to thank Norma McGough BSc Hons FRD for
acting as UK consultant on the series.

....

Editorial Director: LaVonne Carlson
Editors: Nancy Burke, Barbara Minton, Connie Robinson
Designer: Carol Wells
Cover Designer: Gus Yoo

Picture Credits: Steve Gorton, David Murray, Dave King, Martin Norris,
Philip Gatward, Andy Crawford, Philip Dowell, Clive Streeter, Peter Chadwick,
Tim Ridley, Andrew Whittack, Martin Cameron

see our complete catalogue at
www.dk.com

P O C K E T   H E A L E R S

Vitamin D

MAXIMIZING MINERALS

Stephanie Pedersen

A DORLING KINDERSLEY BOOK

CONTENTS